NEW APPRECIATIONS

40

Between the Revolutions:

Russia 1905 to 1917

R. B. McKean

NEW APPRECIATIONS

Published by the Historical Association

EDITOR
Malcolm Crook

DESIGN AND PRODUCTION
Kerina West

© R. B. McKean 1998

Published by the Historical Association and printed in
Great Britain by Blackmore Ltd, Longmead,
Shaftesbury, Dorset SP7 8PX.

NEW APPRECIATIONS

The Historical Association

ISBN 085278 409 0

Contents

A view along the Moskva river to the Kremlin, heart of the capital of Russia
Popperfoto

Introduction

This quotation succinctly expresses the problem that faced both contemporaries and subsequent generations of historians confronting the development of Russia between the revolutions of 1905 and 1917. The upheavals of 1905 and 1906 ostensibly transformed Russia from an absolutist to a constitutional monarchy but, like contemporary observers, historians have disagreed on the extent to which constitutional government was really taking root in Russia. On the one hand 'optimistic' historians have argued that a constructive, peaceful transition towards liberalism and democracy was taking place in the years after 1907. According to this view, there occurred a process of political and social stabilisation, and rapid progress in the direction of Western society. The historic gulf between government and society was finally being bridged. These successful strides along the path of modernisation were cut short only by the Great War. On the other hand, 'pessimistic' histori-ans emphasise the fragility of the new political system and of society in general after 1907. In their view the political and economic reforms initiated by P. A. Stolypin, the President of the Council of Ministers between 1906 and 1911, were not enough to create lasting pacifi-cation and stability. The historic divi-sion between state and society endured because the fundamental sources of dis-affection of peasants, workers and na-tional minorities were not alleviated before 1914. The years from 1911 to 1914 also witnessed the collapse of Stolypin's political system and the recru-descence of labour unrest, now orches-trated by a revitalised Bolshevik party. A new revolutionary crisis was in the making and the Great War merely exac-erbated these re-emergent social tensions.

Any attempt to evaluate the sources of instability and creativity, which were both present in tsarist Russia after 1906, cannot be isolated from the general po-litical, economic and social fissures that became apparent in the decades before 1905. The institutional and legal foun-dations of the constitutional monarchy represent an equally important part of such an assessment. It is with these two topics, therefore, that this pamphlet be-gins.

Russia on the Eve of the 1905 Revolution

The kaleidoscopic upheavals of 1905 to 1907 demonstrated that Russia was facing a crisis of state that was the product of fundamental problems, deeply rooted in economy and society. Russia had experienced an intense but uneven modernisation, beginning with the emancipation of the serfs in 1861 by Alexander II and gathering pace in the 1890s with S. Iu. Witte's state-induced industrial spurt. The imperial government, however, failed to contain economic and social change, and to adapt effectively to it. In particular tsardom refused to alter its archaic and autocratic political structure, a significant cause of the conflict that developed after 1881 between the authorities and an emergent educated public or 'society', demanding civil liberties and a share in the exercise of power.

Until October 1905, imperial Russia was in the formal sense an autocratic, centralised, bureaucratic monarchy in which the tsar exercised supreme and unlimited powers. The monarchy governed with the assistance of five groups: the civil service; the security police; the army; the nobility; and the Russian Orthodox Church. These groups will be examined in turn.

The civil service constituted an autonomous structure superimposed upon the hereditary, landed nobility which, since 1861, had gradually lost its earlier dominant role in the bureaucracy, except in the State Council, the Senate and the Ministries of Justice and the Interior. Yet, because the ruling stratum was drawn from a narrow social, ethnic and religious base, peasants, workers and national minorities still associated the state with the traditional elite.[2] In practice, the Empire was relatively undergoverned, in part due to its enormous size and diversity, financial constraints, and the narrow pool of educated talent on which it could draw. Provincial government lacked a dense network of institutions, whilst the state's principal agents, the provincial governors, proved unamenable to consistent control from the centre. The result was that the countryside was essentially self-administering.

If the Empire was relatively under-administered, the establishment of the security police in 1880 and the introduction of emergency law and order legislation in 1881 ensured that it would be even more arbitrarily governed than before. Nevertheless, though Russia after 1881 can be described as a proto-police state, it was grossly underpoliced. A corrupt, incompetent, and ill-paid police force could not control the countryside in any systematic fashion.

As a consequence of the deficiencies of the police, the imperial army acted as an internal as well as an external defence force. Like the bureaucracy, by the turn of the century the military had ceased to be the private preserve of the landed nobility. Most officers remained politically conservative and loyal to the dynasty, but the numerous mutinies of 1905-6 exposed only too starkly the social and cultural gulf, the mutual distrust, between officers and peasant soldiers.[3]

In social terms, the Romanov monarchy had historically relied upon the loyalty of the landowning nobility, but by the late nineteenth century it no longer commanded the latter's firm support. Older explanations attributed this loss of faith to a steep decline in noble landholding and a rise in noble indebtedness after 1861, as a consequence of the failure of noble landowners to turn themselves into capitalist farmers, the impact of the Great Depression upon agriculture and the challenge of industrialisation. Modern research suggests, however, that there was not a wholesale crisis of the nobility. S. Becker has persuasively argued that many nobles adapted with success to the new economic and social environment. Many larger noble landowners became agrarian entrepreneurs, or moved into the professions, the civil service or the educational world. In the late 1890s and early 1900s, a minority of noble landowners, particularly those who served as members of the zemstvos (the units of local government elected on a narrow franchise) entered politics by participating in the nascent 'liberation movement' for political reform.[4]

Over the centuries the spiritual power of the Russian Orthodox Church had become an intrinsic constituent of popular loyalty to the monarchy. Between the 1860s and 1905, however, the underlying interests of Church and state had come to diverge. Although the secular authorities controlled the Church through the office of the Procurator of the Holy Synod, the Church was a poor instrument of state policy. This was the product of social and economic divisions within the clergy, of the split between a privileged, exclusive and affluent episcopal oligarchy, and the poor, ill-educated parish clergy, which bred a weak sense of loyalty and cohesion within the Church.[5]

These deficiencies in the tsarist system were exacerbated by economic developments occurring at the end of the nineteenth century. The faster tempo of industrialisation in the 1890s, in particular, exerted a profound influence upon a society still legally categorised by estates to 1917. By the 1890s and 1900s social identities were in flux. The older forms of estates were weakening, but had not been completely replaced by new socio-economic classes which might have offered an alternative basis for the regime.

The emergent middle classes were politically splintered and socially fissured. The commercial and industrial middle classes never developed a common mentality, social consciousness, or political allegiance. Ethnic diversity and regional economic rivalries divided entrepreneurs and merchants. Finally, the professional middle class was numerically small, as well as being legally and economically dependent on the state.[6]

The internal security of the Empire ultimately depended on the tranquillity and loyalty of the peasants, who formed the vast bulk of the population of 125 million in 1897. By the 1890s the basic weakness of the state was thus exemplified in the rural crisis. The classic historical explanation of that crisis embraced the impoverishment of the peasantry, a product of the terms of the emancipation of 1861, together with regressive state fiscal policies, a fall in grain prices and rapid population growth. This interpretation has been profoundly modified by recent findings. P. Gregory has demonstrated that agricultural output grew by 2.5 to 3 per cent per annum between 1885 and 1914. As a consequence, rural consumption rose in the long term, outstripping population growth. Peasant purchasing power increased, as is evidenced by the rise in rural savings, land purchases and a slow improvement in diets. The peasant disturbances of 1905-

6 were not, therefore, the product of a uniform decline in rural living standards. They occurred in localities, such as the Central Black Earth and Volga provinces, which had experienced a fall in per capita grain production contrary to the general trend, or among particular groups of peasants such as agricultural labourers. The peasant movement drew its force above all from the peasantry's age-old belief that all the land belonged to God, and from a millenarian expectation of an imminent 'black repartition' or redistribution of all land.[7]

The nascent working class, 70 per cent of which found employment in rural-located rather than urban factories in the

A meeting of a mir, the traditional peasant council made the basic unit of local government by the 1861 reforms
V&A Picture Library

1900s, clearly did not fit into the existing corporate legal structure. Yet the state signally failed to come to terms with this new group. Its labour policies wavered between authoritarian paternalism, repression and Western-style labour relations. Nor did the revolutionary parties, the Social Democrats and the Social Revolutionaries, enjoy any greater success. They never controlled the strike movement in 1905-6.

The 1905 revolution, which exposed so many tensions in tsarist Russia, also brought the nationality question into the open. Embracing some 100 nationalities, the Russian Empire was as much a multi-national state as Austria-Hungary. In general terms the awakening of the nationalities was the product of the policies of Russification, introduced from the 1880s onwards to contain the threat of minority nationalisms. Russification, pursued in an inconsistent and incoherent manner, entailed administrative centralisation in the first instance but, increasingly under Alexander III, it involved conscious attempts to promote Russian language and culture, as well as the Orthodox faith. The danger to the Empire from the centripetal forces of nationalism was less than it appeared, however. The Poles apart, not a single national movement sought outright independence. In 1905-6 national demands did not extend beyond cultural or political autonomy. Indeed, in the case of the Ukrainians and Belorussians, the combination of policies of assimilation and severe repression enjoyed much success, delaying the formation of native intelligentsias and the emergence of ethnic consciousness.

In the last resort, the prestige and domestic authority of the Romanov dynasty was intimately connected to success abroad. The maintenance of Russia's Great Power status was rightly held by tsarist statesmen to be integral to the monarchy's very survival, but the onset of industrialisation, the unification of Germany, and the changing technology of warfare, as well as the state's recurrent financial problems, all threatened to place Russia's international position in jeopardy. Indeed, Russia's diplomatic isolation in the face of the Triple Alliance, after William II of Germany refused to renew the Reinsurance treaty in 1890, drove Russia to make the Dual Alliance with France in 1894. In the same way, fear that time was not on Russia's side if she did not enter the race for colonies, was a major factor behind Witte's drive into a crumbling China in the 1890s. Yet Russia was ready for war neither in Europe nor in Asia, as her disastrous performance in the war which broke out with Japan early in 1904 testified; in 1905, as in 1917, military defeat was the trigger for upheaval.

H.I.M. Nicholas II, Emperor of Russia, by Bogdanow-Bielsky
Royal Collection Enterprises

The Making of the Constitutional Monarchy, 1905-1907

A major characteristic of the constitutional order which emerged from the revolution of 1905 was a lack of definition. The October Manifesto and Fundamental Laws held different meanings for different people. Even their makers were ambivalent about their creations. The explanation of these features of the new political system lay in the ad hoc way the novel institutions had been fashioned by imperial ministers and bureaucrats in response to the fast moving events of 1905 and 1906.[8]

The various political concessions from the tsar and ministers in 1905-6 were not voluntary. They came late and only under pressure. The first, the so-called Bulygin Duma, 6 August 1905, a consultative assembly, was rejected as too limited by the liberal and radical opposition. The second, and more fundamental concession, was the October Manifesto of 17 October 1905. In this brief document, Nicholas II abandoned the principle of autocracy. He promised civil liberties, as well as a genuine legislative body, the State Duma, elected by wider strata of the population than in the electoral law to the Bulygin Duma. Faced by the doubtful loyalty and absence of much of his troops, as well as the general strikes paralysing the urban centres, Nicholas II caved in because he felt he lacked a viable alternative. In the months after October 1905, a series of meetings of the new Council of Ministers, as well as special conferences under the personal chairmanship of the tsar, worked out the powers of the new legislature (Statutes of 20 February 1906). They also devised an amended electoral system (the law of 11 December 1905).

To the surprise and dismay of liberals, the State Duma ceased to be a unicameral body. Determined to secure a conservative counterweight to the popularly elected lower chamber, ministers retained the socially exclusive State Council, the highest consultative body on legislation under the autocracy, as an upper chamber with equal powers to its lower counterpart. The composition of the State Council was reformed to make half its members appointed by the tsar and half elected by separate corporations. The Statutes of 20 February 1906 conferred on both the State Council and State Duma the right to approve all bills and the budget, as well as to interpellate ministers. Bureaucrats' fears of parliamentarism ensured that ministers remained individually responsible to the tsar rather than to the legislature.

Since the Council of Ministers and the tsar rejected the introduction of universal suffrage as leading to the depotism of the masses, the electoral law of 11 December 1905 merely accommodated new categories of voters (mainly the industrial and professional middle classes, as well as factory workers) within the indirect electoral system devised by the electoral law to the Bulygin Duma. Women, over 60 per cent of the working class, agricultural and day labourers, and servants all remained excluded.

Furthermore, fearing the new legislature would arrogate to itself 'constituent' functions, ministers and high officials revised the Fundamental State Laws (1892 version) to incorporate the Statutes of 20 February and published them on 23 April 1906 shortly before the opening of the Duma. The document defined the powers of the Emperor in a sweeping fashion. The Laws' list of civil rights was modest and their exercise was restricted by generalised exceptions though, after some intense debate at a conference held at Tsarskoe Selo, a majority present had persuaded Nicholas II to drop the descriptive adjective 'unlimited' from the definition of his own powers.

The capstone of the constitutional edifice was the electoral law of 3 June 1907, promulgated as a decree by Stolypin upon the dissolution of the Second State Duma. For ministers the electoral wager on a 'conservative' and 'loyal' peasantry (enshrined in the electoral law of 11 December 1905) had proved profoundly misconceived. In the elections both to the First and Second Dumas the peasants had cast their votes for the Kadets and the Trudoviks, who promised to redistribute privately owned land. Thus, the law of 3 June established the political national within considerably narrower electoral limits.[9] By electoral gerrymandering, Stolypin sought to reestablish political stability by granting dominance in the provincial electoral assemblies, which elected the Duma deputies, to the moderately conservative landed nobility.

Nonetheless, the political changes of 1905-6 did not amount to 'false constitutionalism', as is often alleged. Russia ceased to be an unlimited autocracy and became a constitutional monarchy. The powers of the tsar were restricted with the creation of the legislature and the Council of Ministers. The civil freedoms enshrined in the Fundamental Laws marked a definite advance. Admittedly there were flaws in the new constitution. The retention of the definition of the tsar's power as 'autocratic' in article four of the Fundamental Laws imparted a dangerous ambiguity to the new constitutional structure. The promise of the rule of law had still to be fulfilled by concrete legislative guarantees of civil liberties. Yet the very existence of the State Duma created the possibility of a fundamental constitutional shift by non-revolutionary means. The political history of the years after 1907 would provide an indication whether that potential was to be realised or not.

The Third June Political System, 1907-1914

> Reform at a time of revolution is necessary because the shortcomings of the domestic order in large measure spawned the revolt.

P. A. Stolypin, January 1907.[10]

Stolypin, the dominant political personality between 1906 and 1911, was a nobleman who owned large estates in the ethnically mixed western borderlands. This background shaped his political outlook: he was both a monarchist and a Great Russian nationalist. As the quotation illustrates, he was acutely aware that repression was useless unless accompanied by social and political reforms. He wanted to revitalise 'Great Russia' and saw the need to work with the legislature and public opinion. Yet the stabilisation of the new political structure, as well as the lasting pacification of the country, depended not only upon Stolypin's ability to secure firm support for his reforms in parliament, in the bureaucracy and at court, but also upon the institutional, social and civic underpinnings of the system. Chief among the obstacles to Stolypin's conservative modernisation of Russia were the tsar, the State Council, the electoral law of Third June and the fragmentation of Duma politics.

The stamp of provisionality upon the consitutitional order derived from the fact that the tsar, many high officials and extreme conservatives all continued to harbour grave doubts about the dilution of the autocratic system, which they had conceded solely out of necessity. Nicholas II remained ambivalent about the new order. Whilst he played the role of a non-interventionist legalistic monarch until 1911, his retreat derived less from his sincere conversion to constitutionalism than from his reaction to the disasters of his earlier personal rule between 1902 and 1905.

A significant reason for the tsar's non-interference in the affairs of government was that the State Council fulfilled the hopes of its creators. It consistently acted to check 'excessive' reform measures emanating from the lower house. This was because a high proportion of its members came from the conservative, provincial landed nobility. In the years after 1906 the influence of the Right group came to predominate in the upper chamber at the expense of the reformist Centre and Left groups.

In fact, by giving a genuine share of political power to the provincial landed nobility, the electoral law of 3 June 1907 turned out to be one of Stolypin's gravest political miscalculations. At one level the law worked as he intended: 44 per cent of the deputies attending the first session of the Third Duma late in 1907 were of noble origin. Contrary to Stolypin's expectations, however, the moderate conservatism of these noble deputies proved a major hindrance to significant change. This was particularly the case with Stolypin's local government and religious reforms.

In his draft bills for local government, Stolypin endeavoured both to solve the chronic problems of undergovernment and bridge the gap between the state and propertied society, as well as supplant the particularistic system of administration in the countryside.[11] His plans aroused intense opposition from the provincial landed nobility. They believed that the proposals for district government threatened the nobility's local leadership. So effective was noble lobbying in ministerial chancelleries that only one of Stolypin's bills was even presented to parliament. In the case of religious reforms, not a single one of fourteen bills on religious matters ever became law. The leading opponent of concessions to dissenting religious minorities was the hierarchy of the Orthodox Church, which successfully mobilised support among conservative nobles.

Another hallmark of the Duma political system was the proliferation of parties, the absence of a clear majority in the Duma, the decline of extra-parliamentary organisations, and the internal disarray and break-up of the two major parties, the Octobrists and the Nationalists.

Both the Third and Fourth State Dumas contained a multiplicity of parliamentary groupings. There were eleven in the first session of the Third Duma. One reason for this, apart from genuine differences in political views, was the fact that noble deputies from local government tended to regard themselves as independent-minded representatives of their localities. Thus, they held weak political allegiances and shunned party discipline. As a consequence of the large number of parliamentary groups, the Third and Fourth Dumas both lacked a majority, either for reform or for counter-revolution. At the opening of the Third Duma in 1907 the largest party was the Octobrists who, as their name suggests, supported the Manifesto of October 1905, but their 154 deputies fell far short of the requisite Duma majority of 222. Despite large-scale government intervention in the elections to the Fourth Duma in 1912 with the purpose of creating a right-wing majority, neither Right, Centre nor Left enjoyed a preponderance. The result was that Stolypin and his successors could not rely upon a single political or social group to support all of their programmes. The weaknesses of the Duma parties also derived from the fact that they lacked truly national structures. Continual governmental restrictions upon political activities (all parties to the left of the Octobrists were refused legalisation) and the relative indifference of the educated public to party politics after 1907, promoted the atrophy of the parties' provincial branches. In effect the Duma parties and politics were confined to the educated society of St Petersburg and Moscow.

In the light of these circumstances, Stolypin found it increasingly difficult to secure firm foundations of support in the legislature. In the years 1907 to 1911 he relied upon the Octobrists as the largest party in parliament.[11] They proved to be undisciplined allies, who did not provide consistent backing for reforms due to the party's ideological, organisational and social fragility. Although the party leadership, in particular A. I. Guchkov, was committed to the implementation of the promises of the October Manifesto, the majority of its members were Great Russian landed noblemen of conservative beliefs for whom the party's programme meant little. In the face of the Octobrists' irresolution and the continuance of the resistance of the Right to his reforms, from the autumn of 1909 Stolypin reoriented the weight of his domestic policies from reformism to Great Russian nationalism, in order to unite the various sections of the elite and to create a right-wing bloc in the Duma. In this change of tack he was fortuitously aided by the formation in October 1909 of the Nationalist party, an amalgamation of the fractions of the Moderate Right and the Nationalist Group.[13] The Nationalists, with eighty-seven deputies, represented the interests of moderate conservative, Great Russian, progressive landowners in the Western provinces. They sought to promote Great Russian predominance there at the expense of the Polish nobility and the Ukrainian and White Russian peasantry. The Nationalists' hopes of becoming the largest party in parliament were, however, dashed at the elections to the Fourth Duma when they failed to break out of their western heartland and were split by the secession of the more moderate Centre late in 1912.

A major cause of the incoherence of the Duma political system lay in the social fragmentation of Russia in the early twentieth century. The reformed autocracy failed to find support either in surviving estates, or in the classes that were in the process of formation.[14] In the first place, the nobility did not form a unified social class. It was stratified by income and land ownership. It was also divided by ethnicity, religion and occupational allegiances. Thus, Stolypin's attempted political alliance with the provincial landed nobility rested upon a very narrow section of the nobility, perhaps some 20 per cent. Furthermore, the nobility was politically divided after 1906, distributing its loyalties among both Right-and Left-wing parties.

Secondly, the fundamental social weakness of Russian liberalism, the absence of a solid bourgeois core, derived from the social fissures within the emergent middle classes. This prevented the formation of a single party of the entrepreneurial class. After their unsuccessful attempt to enter the new national politics in 1905-6, both the St Petersburg and southern industrialists shunned Duma politics. Although the Progressist party was founded in 1912 by prominent Moscow textile manufacturers with the explicit aim of securing a greater political role for Russia's industrial class, the Progressists utterly failed to unite the merchantry and bridge the gap with the landed nobility and professional intelligentsia.[15] The abstention from political activity by the professions after 1906 also gravely weakened liberalism.

The strength or otherwise of the new political system also depended upon whether the firm preconditions for civil society were being created in the years after 1907. Historians are far from unanimous in their verdict. Some scholars believe that a new public culture was in the process of formation, a 'public sphere' marked by voluntary associations, the expansion of literacy and education, the growth of the professions and a mass press, and the emergence of the State Duma as a forum for political articulation. There was the formation after 1906 of proto-political institutions such as congresses, conferences, educational societies and charities. Discussion and criticism in the press developed into an independent political force.

On the other hand, a powerful case can be made that the political and social structures upon which the emergent civil society rested were not sufficiently solid. The attempt, begun by bureaucratic reformers in 1905-6, to create a *Rechtsstaat*, a state founded upon the rule of law, foundered in the years that followed. The October Manifesto's promises of civil freedoms were never implemented in formal laws. As the history of the trade unions, public congresses and the press illustrates after 1906, police considerations predominated in the implementation of 'temporary regulations'. There was, therefore, a lack of absolute legal guarantees. This was particularly evident in the provinces, where the local authorities suppressed the moderate opposition press and parties as much as the revolutionary ones. There were no improvements in the rights of the national minorities either.

Nor did the renewed monarchy successfully employ the Orthodox Church to strengthen its authority after 1906. Indeed, the Church's ill judged policies actually contributed to a further reduction in the monarchy's support. The Holy Synod and the episcopate signally failed to fashion a coherent, consistent and intelligent policy to defend the regime. Their many blunders aroused much hostility against the government and the Church itself. They made the grave mistake of lending Church support to extreme proto-fascist, anti-Semitic organisations, in particular the Union of Russian People, because these groups were the only unconditional defenders of the Church and the autocracy. Bishops and clergy lost credibility among educated and propertied strata by their association with such unsavoury bodies. The emerging Rasputin scandal in 1911-14 inflicted as much harm on the Church as on the tsar. Rasputin's interference in episcopal appointments from 1912 onwards made the Holy Synod and the episcopate objects of ridicule and contempt.

The government's policies towards the national minorities after the 1905 revolution equally failed to recover their trust. The regime had been terrified by the threat to the Empire's unity posed by the national movements of 1905-6. The aggressive official policies towards the nationalities after 1907 stemmed in part from the conviction of many high officials that the revolution had been the work of non-Russians.[16] Stolypin sincerely believed in the Russian nationalist objectives of his policy. He was committed to the indivisibility of the Empire but, as mentioned earlier, he also deliberately employed nationalist policies from 1909 onwards to bolster his government. His measures were aimed at upholding Great Russian predominance in Poland and the western borderlands, as well as reversing Finland's autonomous constitutional status.[17]

The Finns were the only national minority in 1905-6 to wring significant concessions from the regime. They not only regained their autonomy but secured genuine universal suffrage and civil freedoms. These gains, however, made Stolypin determined to retrieve the powers he believed the imperial government had lost to Finland and to stamp on separatist tendencies. The law of June 1910 thus deprived the Finnish Assembly of its legislative authority, so as to reassert Imperial power in Finland. With regard to Poland, the key measure for both Stolypin and the Nationalists was the bill of 1910 to introduce zemstvos into the western provinces as a device to weaken the position of Polish landowners and to ensure the control of local power by the Great Russian noble landowners. Then in 1912, ostensibly in order to protect the rights of the Russian minority, the Polish district of Kholm was incorporated into Russia proper. The Jewish minority was also a victim of the nationalist backlash. In the light of bureaucrats' beliefs that the Jews were a main force in the revolutionary movement, and right-wing, conservative dominance in the Duma, any relaxation of anti-Jewish legislation was unthinkable. Stolypin's proposed minor concessions of 1906 had been vetoed by Nicholas II and hostile measures increased after 1910. The Western Zemstvo bill denied the vote to Jews, there were increasing expulsions of Jews from outside the Pale of Settlement, and the offensive culminated in the obscene trial of the Jew, Mendel Beilis, wrongfully accused of ritual murder in 1913.

Yet the government was unwilling to pursue a consistent policy of Great Russian nationalism. In the Baltic provinces, for example, it simply maintained the level of administrative and educational Russification achieved by the middle of the 1890s. In the Caucasus, the viceroy, Count V. D. Vorontsov-Dashkov, made real concessions in order to ease ethnic tensions. He restored church lands to the Armenians, whilst he secured passage by the Duma in 1912 of a law abolishing the dues paid by Georgian peasants to their landlords. Both the experiences of 1905, which had raised national consciousness, and the inconsistencies of official policies after 1906 ensured that the support of the national minorities for the Empire was diminished.

The internal contradictions and institutional weaknesses of the Third June political system had manifested themselves before Stolypin's murder in September 1911. Indeed, the crisis which arose from the State Council's rejection of the Western Zemstvo bill in March 1911 had already effectively destroyed Stolypin and his system. In persuading the tsar to use his emergency powers to pass the measure, Stolypin thereby ended his authority at court and in the Duma, as well as alienating the Octobrists who considered the action unconstitutional.

The immediate pre-war years were marked instead by the reappearance of the tsar as a political actor. Nicholas II became increasingly determined to reassert his autocratic prerogatives and to take a more active part in government. To prevent the re-emergence of a high-handed Chairman of the Council of Ministers, the tsar denied Stolypin's two successors, V. N. Kokovtsov (September 1911 - January 1914) and I. L. Goremykin (January 1914 - January

1916), the post of Minister of Internal Affairs. Nicholas also deliberately condoned dissent within the Council. The tsar, therefore, bore a heavy responsibility for the growing disarray at the top of the state structure. Both Kokovtsov and Goremykin proved unable to establish any uniform political direction upon the government. Their cabinets were racked by bitter personal intrigues. Stolypin's successors abandoned all pretence at reform and both lacked a dependable majority in the Duma. Nicholas also supported the reactionary Minister of Internal Affairs, N. A. Maklakov, in his counter-attack against civil and political rights, in particular (early in 1914), parliament's rights of interpellation, legislative initiative and freedom of speech. Ministers did, however, manage to block the tsar's plans to make the Duma a purely consultative body.

The dissipation of the reform ethos after 1911, like the pursuit of openly reactionary causes by certain ministers, led inevitably to the re-emergence of the gulf between state and educated society. Yet the liberal opposition's inability to evolve a coherent and effective response to the gathering forces of reaction also contributed to a growing political deadlock on the eve of the Great War. A cardinal cause of liberalism's weak re-action lay in the fate of the Octobrist party. The imposition of the Western Zemstvo bill struck a fatal blow to Octobrism by destroying its collaboration with the government in the cause of reform. The subsequent attempt of Guchkov, at the party congress of November 1913, to compel his party to adopt a firm oppositional stance led to its complete disintegration. Secondly, the opposition parties - the Octobrists, the Kadets and the Progressists - whilst seeking a legal solution to the political crisis of 1913-14, failed to reach agreement on a common programme, or the use of the budget as a weapon of struggle. The Octobrists feared the dissolution of the Duma, while a majority of Octobrists, Progressists and even Kadets, influenced by Great Russian nationalist sentiments and a growing apprehension of a German threat, could not contemplate the rejection of the 'Great Programme' of military rearmament. Thirdly, Octobrist-Kadet collaboration proved impossible due to mutual distrust. The liberal leaders spurned the call of the left-wing of the Kadets and the Progressist leader, A. I. Konvalov, to mobilise all sectors of society against tsardom through the recreation of the Union of Liberation of 1905. In these circumstances the liberal opposition was doomed to impotence.

Economic and Social Change, 1907-1914

If parliamentary politics after 1907 claimed less and less of the peasantry's attention, the same could not be said of the peasant problem as far as the regime was concerned. It would scarcely be an exaggeration to say that agrarian reform became a matter of life and death for the constitutional monarchy. Long-term political and social stability was bound up with radical changes in rural relations after the widespread rural uprising of 1905-6.

Scholarly judgement on the agrarian reforms, which bear Stolypin's name, but the principles of which had been determined before his accession to power, has undergone drastic revision in the last twenty years.[18] The traditional view emphasised that the purpose of the reforms centred upon the break-up of the commune, which was blamed for agrarian unrest and viewed as an impediment to rural progress. Stolypin, it was argued, sought to strengthen the existing order by creating a new class of medium-sized, conservative landowners. The main thrust of recent monographs, however, is to stress both the mixed goals and evolutionary, gradualist nature of the reforms in response to peasant pressure from below. At first, from 1906 to 1909, political considerations were uppermost in bureaucrats' minds. Stolypin's imme-diate concern was to pacify the countryside, remove the threat to noble landownership and win back peasant support for the monarchy. These desiderata dictated the removal of restrictions upon peasant withdrawal from the commune (the decree of 9 November 1906), a sympathetic response to peasant claims to allotment strips as private property in an integrated plot and the formation of consolidated, owner-occupied farms separate from the commune. As it became increasingly evident to the authorities by 1909-10 that the peasants were on the whole opposed to separated farms, the economic goals of the reformers were accorded greater prominence. These focused upon the modernisation of farming through the consolidation of strips into integral plots within the commune, in order to solve the problem of land fragmentation, so intensifying peasant agriculture and raising productivity. Emphasis shifted to consolidation of strips by individuals or by entire villages, as well as group land settlements.

Scholars are as divided in their evaluation of the agrarian reforms' chances of success as they are of their origins. The suspension of the reforms' implementation at the outbreak of the Great War and the unreliability of the official statistics render a definitive assessment impossible. Any estimation also should bear in mind the distinction between the reforms' political and economic goals.

From the longer-term perspective, the peasant revolt of 1917 threw into stark relief the collapse of the political hopes of the reforms' progenitors. The peasantry's hatred for the landed nobility and desire for the abolition of the latter's estates were in no way allayed by the reforms. Furthermore, peasant resistance to the establishment of separated farms was endemic. In this respect, the individualisation goal clearly failed. By 1915 a mere 300,000 peasant households had set up individual farms outside the commune. The complex of social, economic and psychological ties binding village communes together proved a real block. Thus, by 1917, around three-quarters of peasants still lived in communes. Whilst there was no repeat of the peasant disturbances of 1905-6, growing rural hooliganism in the years preceding the war hinted at intense peasant discomfort under the surface.

On the other hand, the reforms were beginning to bear fruit with regard to their economic objectives. Peasants might have rejected physical dispersal of their villages, but they were increasingly prepared to countenance the establishment of enclosed farms within the villages or, even more so, group land settlements. By 1914 about half of all peasant households had requested some form of governmental assistance in reorganising their holdings. The frequency of peasant land purchases, individually or collectively, increased after 1905. The government transferred millions of acres of state land to the Peasant Land Bank, which also purchased the estates of nobles fleeing the countryside after 1905. The Bank sold over twelve million acres of land to peasants between 1909 and 1915. The development of Siberia, too, was an integral part of the reforms. Stolypin actively sponsored emigration from the overpopulated provinces of European Russia. Almost five million peasants were resettled between 1904 and 1913, mainly in Western Siberia, where they were given large, consolidated farms. The migrants' prosperity rested upon the rapid development of animal husbandry and the export of dairy produce. A sign of increasing peasant self-reliance was the swift growth of the rural co-operative movement after 1906, particularly in Siberia. Geographically, however, the economic impact of the agrarian reforms was uneven. It was least effective in the Central Black Earth provinces, which remained a region of overpopulation and economic distress.

Taking the broader perspective of the agrarian economy after 1907, the long-term increase in grain output was maintained. After a decline in output in 1905-8, grain production grew by four per cent per annum between 1909 and 1913, leading to a significant rise in grain exports. The long-term improvement in peasant living standards continued, attested by the rise in peasants' savings. These general advances, however, concealed sectoral and regional weaknesses. The number of livestock per head of population may actually have declined. Regional grain imbalances increased before 1914. The output of grain per head of the population fell in the Central Black Earth and Volga regions.

In the years immediately preceding 1914, the prospects for industry were as bright as for agriculture. Older investi-

Russian settlers in Siberia at the end of the century
National Museum of Finland

gations of the industrial economy advanced the thesis that an autonomous internal market was developing after 1907 with the retreat of the state from economic intervention. Pre-war industrial expansion was seen as the product of an increase in consumer spending due to rising peasant prosperity, but recent research suggests that the transformation in the pattern of industrial development after 1907 has been exaggerated.

After the 'economic miracle' of the 1890s, industry had endured a limited depression between 1900 and 1903. The revolution of 1905 led to a major decline in output, with three years of negative growth thereafter. Recovery set in from 1910. Between both 1905-9 and 1909-13, net national product grew by almost 5 per cent per annum and net investment by over 11 per cent per annum. This boom was the product of both autonomous and state-induced forces. In the case of the former, there was the rapid expansion of the consumer goods industries. The role of foreign savings in financing domestic investment fell in comparison to the late 1890s. On the other hand, although the state played a smaller part as an investor, it continued to make a significant contribution as a consumer. In the case of the capital goods industries, state orders remained highly relevant to their fortunes. The capital goods sector was the beneficiary of rearmament and of new state orders for railway rolling stock after 1911. Foreign capital, furthermore, was still dominant in new industries like electrical engineering. Foreign investment was redirected as well into the fast expanding private banking sector. After 1909, close links developed between the joint-stock investment banks and heavy industry, particularly those companies engaged in fulfilling defence orders.

In general terms, Russia was changing from an underdeveloped to a developing society before the Great War. In 1913, Russia was the fourth largest economy in the world. There was a clear dichotomy, however, between her aggregate economic power and continued relative poverty on a per capita basis. On the eve of war, Russian per capita income was a third of France's and a quarter of Germany's. Despite the great industrial boom, Russia's economic power remained concentrated in her agricultural sector. Between 1909 and 1913 agriculture accounted for half of national income, whilst grain alone was responsible for 40 per cent of the value of exports. Russia lagged behind as a serious industrial competitor.

A Revolutionary Challenge, 1911-1914?

As with the peasantry, so with the working class; the defeat of 1905 furnished the regime with an opportunity to win back the loyalty of workers by establishing a new system of industrial relations, based upon the West European model of legal trade unions and collective bargaining. In the event, the failure of both state and employers to forge a coherent labour policy ensured that an alienated working class proved the single most important, if ultimately ineffective, source of opposition to the monarchy after 1907.[19]

The attitude of senior bureaucrats towards labour after 1905 was characterised by ambiguity. The electoral laws of 1905 and 1907 bestowed the franchise on a section of the working population, while the Temporary Regulations of 4 March 1906 allowed the formation of trade unions. The insurance law of 23 June 1912, as well as instituting payments to workers for injuries or illness at work, permitted workers a share in running insurance funds, set up to implement the law's provisions. Political circumstances, however, were detrimental to the reformist option. Though the Ministry of Trade and Industry defended state-directed paternalism, it found little support within the bureaucracy. The Ministry of Inter-

nal Affairs and the Department of Police, which contributed most to labour policy-making, continued to fear independent working-class activity and the use that the revolutionaries might make of legal labour institutions. Indeed, after June 1907, these two agencies launched a campaign, eagerly supported by the employers, to destroy the trade unions which had sprung up in profusion in the previous two years. Between 1906 and 1910, 497 trade unions were closed down and 604 denied registration by the authorities. Such short-sighed policies reinforced the monarchy's identification in workers' eyes as a firm ally of the employers.

Even the economic boom of 1910-14 produced only a feeble trade union resurgence. At their peak in 1907, trade unions claimed 245,335 members; by 1913, a paltry 31,266. Those trade unions which survived were predominantly the preserve of skilled male workers, both factory and artisanal; they failed to attract female operatives, the semi-skilled and the unskilled. On account of their miniscule membership, trade unions were organisationally and financially weak, unable to provide leadership to their members over pay and conditions.

The revolutionary parties fared no better than trade unions in the years immediately after 1907. In the Ukraine, for example, nominal membership of the Russian Social Democratic Party fell from 20,000 in 1906 to a derisory 200 in 1912, and in Moscow from 7,500 to 400. Social, economic and political factors explained this precipitous decline. The depression in industry compelled industrialists to cost-cutting policies, so rescinding the workers' 1905 gains in shorter hours, higher wages and the institution of the 'constitutional' factory order. The steep rise in unemployment and the success of the employers' counter-offensive led inevitably to a decline in workers' morale. Another factor was the effectiveness of the secret police's network of agents within all revolutionary factions, which enabled it to repeatedly smash revolutionary cells. A great part of the intelligentsia, disillusioned by the failure of 1905, abandoned revolutionary activity. All the revolutionary parties, furthermore, were severely weakened after 1907 by internal, ideological divisions over their leaders' response to defeat in revolution and over the use the parties should make of the new legal opportunities. Within Bolshevism, for example, Lenin and his adherents were only one of several factions. These developments entailed profound consequences for the revolutionary parties. Not one revolutionary party established viable, lasting underground networks. All failed to set up national, regional or all-city organisations. They maintained at best a cellular existence in individual factories or workshops. The socialist groups were woefully short of finance, of secret printing presses and illegal literature. None of the exiled leaders abroad, including Lenin, exercised effective control over their parties within Russia. The real leaders of the legal and illegal socialist organisations were the local labour activists or revolutionary sub-elite. Due to the flight of the intelligentsia, these were skilled, male workers or worker-intellectuals. Noted for their antipathy to the sterile factionalism which abosrbed the émigrés' attention, they primarily sought party unity. Indeed, locally, the revolutionary groups tended to co-operate, irrespective of ideological differences.

By contrast, the immediate pre-war period of 1912 to 1914 was noteworthy for the apparent revival of Bolshevik, particularly Leninist, fortunes. In both St Petersburg and Moscow the Bolsheviks succeeded in taking over many of the legal labour institutions from their erstwhile Menshevik leaders. In the elections to the Fourth Duma in 1912, the Bolsheviks secured the six workers' deputies from purely working-class electoral districts. Their newspaper, *Pravda (The Truth)*, launched in April 1912, enjoyed a much higher circulation than its Menshevik rival, *Luch (The Ray)*. In 1913-14 the Bolsheviks succeeded in ejecting the Mensheviks from the boards of the main trade unions in both capitals. Lenin forced a schism in the hitherto united socialist group in the Duma in the autumn of 1913. The Bolsheviks won the elections of labour representatives to the Insurance Council and St Petersburg Insurance Board in 1914. In Georgia alone did Menshevism continue to hold undisputed sway among politically active workers. This decline in sympathy among skilled workers for Menshevism in 1912-14, like growing support for the Bolsheviks' extreme tactics and ideals, owed much to the discrediting of the legal, gradual, peaceful path to change, advocated by the Mensheviks, and to the repressive policies of the state and the employers. The Mensheviks' hostility to the 'strike disease' also did grave damage to their revolutionary credentials.

Yet the Bolsheviks' gains were somewhat illusory and proved very short-lived. In the Fourth Duma elections, for example, the Bolsheviks were aided by the Socialist Revolutionaries' boycott of the polls. In four of the six seats won by Bolsheviks, the electors gave their deputies mandates demanding the restoration of party unity. Only a minority of operatives read the socialist press; most preferred the new daily, popular mass circulation newspapers. The functions of the insurance funds were severely restricted by the authorities and the employers. Workers in general were apathetic towards parliamentary affairs. The trade unions failed to form a broad popular base for any revolutionary party. In short, the legal labour institutions proved to be a feeble vehicle of revolutionary leadership and outreach to the masses. They were unable to act as surrogates for the Bolshevik underground which, in common with all other socialist groups, continued in the same state of near paralysis after 1911 as before, and for the same reasons.

Due to the frailties of the revolutionary parties and the legal labour institutions, the main form of opposition on the part of labour to the monarchy after 1907 was the strike. There had been a steep decline in labour stoppages between 1907 and 1911, until the shooting of unarmed demonstrators at the Lena gold fields on 4 April 1912, so reminiscent of Bloody Sunday, sparked off an ever-increasing tempo of strikes. According to the far from complete data of the factory inspectorate, the number of strikers in the Empire rose from 105,100 in 1911 to 725,491 in 1912 to 887,096 in 1913, reaching a peak of 1,448,684 in the first seven months of 1914. Several features of this renewed upsurge of industrial unrest were significantly different from the last great outburst of labour discontent in 1905-7. In the first place, the unrest was a purely urban phenomenon, concentrated in provinces with urban centres whose population exceeded 200,000 inhabitants. Secondly, it was limited in its geographical scope. St Petersburg city and province was by far the worst affected region, furnishing three-quarters of all strikers between 1912 and 1914. Thirdly, labour disputes remained disproportionately concentrated among certain strata of workers. Between 1912 and 1914 the skilled, better-paid and well-educated metal workers accounted for around half of all strikers. Finally, political protests predominated over stoppages with economic causes. In St Petersburg, the majority of walkouts were of a political nature, overwhelmingly in the metalworking sector. These political strikes provided the main outlet for a diffuse and growing opposition to the regime by more and more workers in the capital, and to a limited extent elsewhere. They bore eloquent testimony to the failure of the political concessions of 1905-6 to pacify the working class.

A conjuncture of circumstances explains this renewed outburst of labour protest. The explosiveness of labour discontent was a belated reaction in part to the employers' counter-offensive after

1907 and to the annulment of the economic achievements of 1905-6. Thus, the restoration of the 'autocratic' factory order proved a prime spur to disaffection. Workers were also able to take the offensive due to the economic recovery that began 1911. The market upsurge created the conditions of low unemployment and an acute shortage of skilled labour favourable to workers to press for improved conditions. The bitter resistance of employers, particularly those organised in the St Petersburg Society of Mill and Factory Owners, and the repressive measures to which they resorted to break strikes, such as fines, lockouts and blacklists, added much fuel to the fire of operatives' anger and opposition. Even in stoppages of an economic nature, which accounted for the majority of working days lost, workers experienced a rising proportion of defeats.

These developments in the labour movement after 1912 seemed to foreshadow a prolonged period of instability in the cities. Yet the danger to the Empire from a pre-war strike movement was less than it seemed. St Petersburg's vanguard role was as much a cause of the movement's weakness as its strength. Geographically and sectorally the new upsurge of labour protest was very limited in comparison with the upheaval of 1905 to 1907. Even in 1914 no more than 12 per cent of all enterprises in Russia under the purview of the factory inspectorate experienced withdrawal of labour. All other branches of manufacturing lagged far behind the metal trades in strike propensity, even including St Petersburg. The so-called 'general strike', which afflicted the capital in the first half of July 1914, in fact involved no more than a quarter of its manufacturing work-force. Above all, enfeebled trade unions and emasculated, illegal, revolutionary parties, not excepting the Bolsheviks, were in no position to guide the working-class opposition as expressed in political protest strikes into mass support for the programmatic demands of the revolutionary parties. The Bolsheviks failed in their commitment to launch a national general political strike, or spark mass street demonstrations, or recreate a Soviet of Workers'Deputies on the model of 1905. They enjoyed no success whatsoever in subverting army garrisons or the fleet. The conclusion must be that from 1912 to 1914 the state and the employers did successfully contain labour protest, through a combination of savage repression and minimal concessions.

Russia as a Great Power, 1907-1914

Although the most immediate threat to the constitutional monarchy seemed to derive from urban labour discontent before 1914, the fate of the regime was ultimately dependent upon the foreign policy pursued by the statesmen of renovated Russia. After 1905, the tsar, Stolypin, ministers and generals were well aware of the links between domestic politics and foreign policy. They believed that the domestic upheavals of 1905-7 had been sparked by participation and defeat in the Russo-Japanese war. They also understood that the armed forces' inglorious performance in Manchuria and the disaffection displayed by soldiers and sailors in 1905-6 made military reform a pressing issue. The quality of the Empire's armed forces was clearly integral to the maintenance of her status as a Great Power.

After 1907 the government and its Ministers of War made great strides towards military recovery and reform.[20] Total defence spending rose from 680 million roubles in 1907 to 961 million roubles in 1913. Among the improvements implemented were: a shortened term of service; a short-lived Council of State Defence, intended to unify military and naval planning; and the territorial system of recruitment and a secret cadre system, introduced in 1910. Nicholas II's support proved crucial to making naval rearmament a top priority after 1906: the small naval programme of 1907 and the 'enhanced programme' of 1912, both expanded the Baltic fleet. The Great Army Programme of 1913-14, a product of the Balkan wars and the increase in the size of the German army, subsequently aimed to raise the army's complement by half a million men and 11,000 officers.

The requirements of military recovery, the country's financial debility, and domestic reconstruction after 1905 all depended, as tsarist statesmen realised, upon the absence of international complications or conflict. The ruling elite was in agreement that Russia must now pursue a pacific, conservative foreign policy. A future war, the bureaucratic consensus ran, would re-ignite the flames of revolution at home.

The conduct of Russia's external relations after 1907 was powerfully moulded by these considerations.[21] Thus, for example, in fashioning the Anglo-Russian entente and the agreement with Japan in 1907, a prime motive of the Minister of Foreign Affairs, A. P. Izvolskii, was to eliminate potential complications in Asia, as well as to overcome the risk of strategic encirclement. In the Bosnian crisis of 1908-9, due to her military weakness and fear that war would revive domestic unrest, Russia was compelled to accept

Germany's veiled ultimatum and to recognise unequivocally Austria-Hungary's annexation of Bosnia-Herzegovina. In their foreign policies, both Izvolskii and his successor, A. D. Sazonov, sought to remain on friendly terms with all the Great Powers. Both men attempted to maintain a balance between the Dual Alliance with France and good relations with Germany.

Yet the fact remains that in July 1914, Russian statesmen consciously pursued a course which ran the risk of war. The reasons they did so illuminate powerful underlying influences which ultimately negated the earlier, sensible pursuit of a strategy of peace.

In the first place, after 1906 Russia could not opt out of being a Great Power nor withdraw from competition with her Great Power rivals. Nicholas II and the elite were firmly committed to keeping Russia a first-class Great Power. They were aware that defeat in war or diplomacy could further weaken the regime. Russia needed diplomatic victories to restore her prestige. In the July crisis of 1914, memories of Germany's abasement of Russia over Bosnia in 1909 played a great role in the minds of Russian statesmen. They believed that if Russia did not respond, she would vacate her position as a Great Power; a second diplomatic disaster could equally damage the state's authority at home.

Secondly, after 1906, fundamental geopolitical, diplomatic and military considerations kept Russia tied to the Dual Alliance. Russian statesmen believed that a united Germany represented a major threat to Russia's Great Power status. By 1913-14, distrust of Germany had become even stronger than loathing of Austria-Hungary due to the apparent German influence in Turkey. In the summer of 1914, Russian ministers and generals became convinced that Germany had connived at Austria-Hungary's actions against Serbia and that Germany sought hegemony in Europe through aggression.

Thirdly, there was considerable agreement about the fundamental premises of the state's foreign policy between the regime and educated society, as represented by the liberal and moderate right-wing parties. Russian nationalism, in particular its Pan-Slav or Neo-Slav components, served as a strong link between them. The Nationalists, the Octobrists, the Progressists and many Kadets felt a common sympathy with the Slav peoples of the Balkans and perceived a growing threat to Russian security from the Central Powers. In the light of these developments, the government could be relatively confident in July 1914 that educated society would support its more belligerent stance against the pretensions of the Germanic powers.

The Military, Economic and Social Impact of the First World War

Whatever the differences among scholars concerning the monarchy's prospects for political and social stability between 1912 and 1914, there is general agreement that the First World War strained the structures of the constitutional monarchy to breaking point. An earlier generation of Western historians emphasised the gross mismanagement of Russia's war effort, both military and economic, by tsarist bureaucrats and generals. [22] Recent reassessments of Russia's military and economic performance, however, have come to more nuanced conclusions, revealing significant successes as well as failures.

In political terms, the impact of the war upon the army was the most disastrous consequence of the three years' hostilities. In a variety of ways, the Great War gradually broke the army's loyalty.[23]

The basic problem faced by Russia's armed forces was that, in common with all other belligerents, the military planners had envisaged only a short war, and miscalculated their requirements for *materiél*. As a consequence, the performance of the armed forces fluctuated considerably. After the initial, disastrous defeat at Tannenberg in East Prussia in August 1914, the army conquered Galicia from Austria-Hungary. Then, in the spring and summer of 1915, the combination of a German attack on Poland, munitions shortages, poor tactics and inept leadership forced Russia out of Poland and Galicia. In 1916, however, the combat capability of the army was restored. Due to the relative success of state-induced industrial reorganisation, the deficiencies in munitions were repaired, giving Russia superiority in men and *materiél* over the Central Powers. In spring 1916, General A. A. Brussilov achieved a stunning tactical victory in Galicia. Russia also made great conquests in eastern Turkey.

These successes were bought at a high price. Casualties were considerable. By 1917 they may have reached some seven and a half million, including nearly two and a half million prisoners of war and almost two million killed or wounded. In an army whose overwhelmingly peasant soldiers lacked a sense of patriotism, this human suffering, combined with the earlier disasters, led to a decline in morale by late 1916, expressed in malingering and dumb insolence. Nevertheless, the front-line army remained intact on the eve of the February revolution; desertions were low. The real military danger to the dynasty, as February 1917 revealed, came from the large numbers of urban training barracks in the rear, composed of poorly disciplined raw recruits. Equally ominous was the fact that the rapid expansion of the officer corps had been met at the expense of radically altering its social composition with the rapid promotion of subalterns of peasant and lower middle-class extraction. By 1917 only 10 per cent of pre-war officers remained with the army. Old ideals of service and loyalty were fatally weakened. By late 1916 the most acute problem was also the least visible. The authorities were running out of men.

The efforts of the government to mobilise the economy for war production met with greater success than contemporary critics and subsequent generations of scholars have been willing to admit. The much criticised officials of tsarist Russia proved able to supply the fiscal and material sinews of war, but at a cost which contributed to the undermining of the regime's authority, and to an increase in existing social tensions in urban and rural areas.

Agriculture performed reasonably well in the first two years of the war. Initial grain-supply problems were not due to any shortfall in production. Despite the conscription of one in two able-bodied rural males and a tenth of all horses, peasant agriculture produced a grain surplus in 1914 and 1915, due to the more intensive use of family labour. Both 1916 and 1917, however, witnessed an actual reduction in total grain output due to reduced sowings and lower yields. By 1916 peasants, whose incomes actually rose during the war, were increasingly reluctant to market their grain for a variety of reasons. The fixed prices set by the state for procurement by the army discouraged sales. There was a growing dearth of consumer goods for sale in the villages and the rouble was also declining in value. Furthermore, large-scale noble farming underwent a severe contraction by 1916, when sowings on private estates fell by a tenth, on account of a drastic reduction in hired labour and a severe contraction both in the domestic manufacture and the imports of agricultural machinery and artificial fertilisers. The fundamental damage to urban food supplies was caused by the fact that the war threw into chaos the traditional patterns of production and consumption, which completely broke down in 1916 and 1917.

The outbreak of war also inflicted tremendous handicaps on industry. It lost important imports, such as coal and cotton. The initial mobilisations granted no exemptions to skilled operatives or miners. Domestic output of coal scarcely rose at all in the war, whilst the supply of metals never kept pace with demand. The disruption of the railways entailed irregular deliveries of raw materials to manufacturers. Nevertheless, the large private firms and monopolies in heavy industry proved capable of adaptation to the needs of modern warfare. Enormous sums were spent on expanding and modernising plant in the defence industries. Women, juveniles, refugees and prisoners of war took the place of factory workers called to the colours. As a consequence, by 1916 output in the capital goods industries was 60 per cent above its 1913 level, greatly augmenting the supply of munitions to the front. This success was dearly bought. The increasing diversion of scarce funds and raw materials to the defence industries by the new state regulatory apparatus meant that the civilian economy, relatively protected for the first two years of the war, suffered in late 1915 and 1916 from a growing shortage of finished goods.

Awarding credit for the relatively successful organisation of war production has been a matter of bitter dispute ever since the Great War. The government's liberal opponents and many historians since have ascribed it to the 'self-activity' of educated society, in particular to the Central War Industries Committee and its regional offshoots. These were founded in the summer of 1915 by Moscow industrialists, genuinely concerned for their country's safety, as well as a share in profitable war orders. In fact, unprecedented state intervention in the realm of private enterprise was the major factor. In August 1915 the government established Special Councils on Defence, Food Supply, Fuel and Transport, bureaucratic organs embracing as well representatives of parliament and the voluntary organisations with wide powers of intervention. The Special Council on Defence, rather than the Central War Industries Committee, became the directing force in the distribution of contracts, finance and raw materials to heavy industry.

The state's method of financing the war, however, had disastrous consequences. The closure of the Baltic by Germany and of the Dardanelles by Turkey at the start of the war devastated exports, turning the pre-war surplus in the balance of trade into a deficit. Facing a reduction in traditional sources of revenue, such as customs dues and the sale of vodka (prohibition was introduced in August 1914), the government covered the massive rise in war expenditure by borrowing. By 1916, two-thirds of expenditure was met in this way. The results were inflationary. The enormous growth in the quantity of incovertible paper currency in circulation led to the depreciation of the rouble.

The social consequences of the war were felt most acutely and were most visible in the cities and towns of the Empire. The increase in the urban population by a quarter between 1914 and 1916 stemmed from an influx of refugees as well as the expansion of industry. When Germany invaded Poland in the summer of 1915, General Headquarters adopted a deluded scorched-earth policy in its retreat. By spring 1916 over three million refugees had fled into the interior. During the wartime boom, employment in large-scale industry increased whilst small-scale industry registered a decline of some 20 per cent. The social composition of the industrial work force altered with the number of women employed in large-scale industry increasing by two-thirds. The war, too, witnessed an acceleration in the concentration of industrial production, lengthening the working day and producing a rise in occupational illnesses and accidents. The sharp addition to the urban population put a severe strain upon already inadequate housing facilities, causing urban rents to double or even treble. The breakdown in trade between town and country, the refusal of the government to introduce rationing for civilians, even for essential foodstuffs, before the autumn of 1916, and the growing congestion of the railway system, conspired to bring about an acute shortage of prime necessities and escalating prices in the urban centres.

Although all groups of workers experienced an upsurge in money wages during the war, metal and chemical operatives alone enjoyed a continuous improvement in real wages to the autumn of 1916; all other industrial categories suffered a precipitate decline in real income from August 1914. For the first time, middle-class income endured a similar fate. The gradual disintegration of the urban social and economic fabric immeasurably strengthened the tempo of both middle-class and working-class alienation from the monarchy. It was no accident, therefore, that the February revolution of 1917 was essentially an urban phenomenon. Their loyalty sapped by deprivation, declining incomes, the irregular appearance of food and fuel and the endless queues, the cities finally revolted.

The Political Impact of the First World War

The influence of the Great War upon Russian politics initially seemed benign. The emergent pre-war consensus between government and educated society concerning the manner and purpose of Russian foreign policy was now confirmed. There was agreement upon the preservation of the Empire's independence, the deliverance of the Balkan Slavs from the Teutonic yoke, and the conquest of Constantinople. Liberals deluded themselves that a spontaneous fervour of patriotism affecting all classes heralded the miraculous advent of a 'Sacred Union', healing the divisions of political and class conflict. Hence, at the sitting of the Duma on 26 July 1914, all the liberal opposition parties, including the Kadets, joined their right-wing colleagues in voting war credits without attaching any conditions. In the same patriotic spirit, liberals rushed to found voluntary organisations to aid the war effort. The Union of Zemstvos and the Union of Towns quickly came to provide the greater part of all medical aid at the front and in the rear for sick and wounded soldiers.

During the first months of hostilities, however, the popularity of the government was irredeemably damaged by the autonomy granted to General Headquarters by the Field Regulations of 16 July 1914. In the absence of the tsar as commander-in chief, which was envisaged by the document, General Headquarters was totally independent of the Ministry of War and the Council of Ministers. As General Headquarters controlled all civilian offices at the front, its arbitrary and repressive policies and incompetent interference soon alienated many people. Its autonomy rendered the pursuit of co-ordinated policies impossible.

In the spring and early summer of 1915 the patriotic union came under increasing strain. The liberals discovered to their dismay that the government intended to continue its reactionary course at home. Distrusting public initiative, ministers hoped to conduct the war without recourse to parliament or collaboration with society. The military disasters and shell shortages both strengthened liberals' belief in the incompetence of an arbitrary administration and their assumption that public activity, as represented by the voluntary organisations, was superior and more efficient. The result was to be the renewal from July 1915 of the struggle between government and educated society.

The political crisis which duly erupted in the summer of 1915 assumed two forms. In the first place, in early August 1915, Nicholas II astonished his ministers, who had not been consulted, by his decision to remove his uncle, the Grand Duke Nikolai Nikolaevich, as supreme commander and assume the post himself. It has recently, and convincingly, been argued that this decision, taken by the tsar due to a mystical sense of duty, was not as ill-conceived as contemporaries and historians have hitherto assumed.[24] It removed a proven incompetent at the head of the army, whilst preventing General Headquarters becoming a rival centre of political power. It was the one way to reunify the fractured military and civilian authority. Nonetheless, the announcement aroused a storm of protest from both ministers and liberals.

Secondly, when the Duma reconvened in July 1915, the liberals advanced the demand for a 'government of confidence', a cabinet composed of the representatives of the bureaucracy and the public, responsible to the tsar. The disintegration of the Octobrists on the eve of the war, as well as the Nationalists' split in August 1915, left the Kadets, despite their small numbers (fifty-one deputies) as the fulcrum of parliamentary politics. The Kadet leader, P. N. Miliukov, succeeded, in August 1915, in the hitherto impossible task of forming a right-centre majority in the Duma. This so-called 'Progressive Bloc' comprised an alliance of Octobrists, Progressists, Kadets and Progressive Nationalists. Miliukov believed that the Bloc, by its very moderation and its visible patriotism, would persuade ministers and tsar to grant a ministry of confidence. His calculations, however, went badly awry. Both Nicholas II and Goremykin shrewdly outmanouevred the incipient coalition between the Bloc and a majority of ministers, who sought accommodation with educated society. The tsar refused further concessions: he believed, not without some basis in fact, that the Bloc's pressure for a ministry of confidence concealed the major constitutional goal of a ministry responsible to parliament. On 3 September 1915, accordingly, the tsar prorogued the Duma.

Despite his honourable motives, Nicholas's departure for the front early in the autumn hastened the decomposition of his government. Both his rejection of the Bloc's programme and his lengthy sojourns at Mogilev, where General Headquarters was located, left him isolated from almost all political and social groups. In his absence, the Empress Alexandra, a confirmed partisan of undiluted autocracy, assumed for the first time a central position in high politics. Her naivety, ignorance of politics and economics, not to mention her psychological dependence on Rasputin, all combined to open the path of advancement to ambitious careerists. Although the infamous 'ministerial leapfrog' in the last seventeen months of the monarchy's existence did in fact see the appointment of some capable as well as some unsavoury and incompetent ministers, it dealt a fatal blow to any semblance of unity in the Council of Ministers or continuity in most fields of policy. These effects were made worse by the complete absence of leadership on the part of Goremykin's successor, B. V. Sturmer, an elderly courtier patently out of his depth in high office. Sturmer's administration abandoned any pretence at seeking constructive collaboration with the Duma or the voluntary organisations. It launched a counter-attack against the latter, seeking to curtail their powers and influence.

Whilst the heightened Great Russian nationalism aroused by the war had its positive features, it also assumed a much darker character. As defeats and shortages mounted in 1915, the regime and much of the populace sought scapegoats in Jews and Germans. The army high command in particular became obsessed with Jews as spies and speculators, producing pogroms and forcible evacuation of whole Jewish communities from the front. Bureaucrats pursued rabidly chauvinistic, anti-German policies. Economic measures were enacted early in 1915 to rid Russia of the so-called 'German Yoke'. The Ukrainians of occupied Galicia also experienced severe persecution at the hands of the Russian military government. Nevertheless, reasons of state could lead on occasions to significant moderation of this extreme stance. In August 1915, for example, a combination of Allied pressure and the sheer numbers of Jewish refugees flooding into the interior, forced the Council of Ministers to grant Jews the right of abode in the towns of inner Russia. In Finland, too, the 'Russification programme' of autumn 1914 was put on ice.

By the autumn of 1916 both popular and elite discontent focused upon the monarchy. The visible disorganisation of the administration, the mounting shortages in the cities, the scandals surrounding Rasputin, the ill-founded rumours of a 'pro-German' party at court seeking a separate peace and the 'treachery' of the Empress, all dealt a severe moral blow to the dynasty. Even the conservatives in the State Council and United Nobility passed resolutions demanding a government in which people could have confidence. As a result of Rasputin's continued scandalous interference in ecclesiastical appointments, the bulk of the episcopate, as well as a majority of priests, had also withdrawn their support from the tsar.

In 1916 the reaction of the liberal Progressive Bloc to these developments was dictated above all by concern for its own unity and survival. The Bloc was inherently fissiparous. Its deliberately imprecise and compromise programme, which had little relevance to the war effort, merely fuelled inner tensions. Fearful both of inciting mass revolt and of a dissolution of the Duma, with new 'managed' elections, the Bloc's leaders stuck to parliamentary tactics. Indeed the Bloc was trapped both by its artificial character and its patriotism. It could scarcely refuse to vote for war credits. Equally unthinkable to the Bloc's strategists was the adoption of a leftward, extra-parliamentary course, as advocated by the left-wing of the Kadets and Progressist industrialists, who urged their colleagues in vain to establish ties with the revolutionary left and the working class. Although the Moscow leadership of the Central War Industries Committee did indeed endeavour to implement their own political programme through the formation of Labour Groups attached to the Committees, their policy met with minimal success, due in part to the hostility of most of their fellow industrialists. It was a measure of the liberals' increasing despair rather than strength that they resorted to spreading widely in printed material the rumours about the Empress and Rasputin, in order to damage the monarchy's prestige, and even to plotting palace *coups*.

Early in 1917, as on the eve of the war, the regime did not face its most immediate danger from the liberal opposition, but from the urban workers. For the revolutionary socialist parties the war, with its defeats, losses and shortages, should have opened up alluring prospects. Yet all the revolutionary factions failed to make the most of them. They proved unable to provide effective leadership for a profound, if diffuse, popular dissatisfaction with the regime. The radicalisation of the working class in the war, therefore, owed little to the endeavours of the revolutionary parties. It was the product rather of the war-induced economic and social dislocations of urban life and of the political crisis within the ruling elite.

A major cause of the revolutionary parties' lack of success lay in pre-war ideological divisions, which were now overlaid by the socialists' response to the outbreak of war. These led to new alignments cutting across existing factional loyalties. Within Bolshevism, for example, it was Lenin's espousal of Russian defeat, as much as the difficulties of wartime communications, which ensured that his influence over Bolsheviks in Russia, most of whom disagreed with his stance on the war, was minimal. The doctrinal hostility shown by most of the socialist factions to the Labour Groups of the War Industries Committees also proved a costly error.

A second factor in the revolutionaries' failure to create a mass, organised anti-war socialist movement was the frailty of their underground organisation. On the eve of the war, the secret police had deprived the revolutionaries of almost all legal means of existence by closing down the legal socialist press and most trade unions. None of the socialist factions, mercilessly persecuted by the police, possessed institutional mechanisms capable of furnishing effective leadership. Revolutionary organisations existed only fleetingly at the level of factory cells. Party allegiance remained slight. Bolshevism, let alone Leninism, failed to predominate within Russian Social Democracy, or the broader socialist and labour movements.

During the war, as in the years after 1907, work stoppages continued to be the most visible source of opposition to the monarchy, and the most significant form of the labour movement in the absence of legal labour organisations and a permanent revolutionary underground. Whilst labour unrest faded away in the second half of 1914, it re-emerged in the spring of 1915. The factory inspectorate recorded a mere 35,000 strikers between August and December 1914, increasing to 539,000 the following year and to 957,000 in 1916.

There were both similarities with and differences from earlier waves of stoppages. The incidence of industrial disputes remained below that of 1905-7 and 1912 - 14. Nor did Petrograd, as the capital was renamed at the outbreak of war, dominate the national strike movement to the same extent as before. In 1915, Moscow and Vladimir provinces witnessed more disturbances, although in 1916 Petrograd province furnished 56 per cent of all strikers. On the other hand, the capital still led Russia in the propensity to strike for reasons of political protest. In Petrograd, such stoppages accounted for two-thirds of all strikes between August 1914 and 22 February 1917, whilst its metalworkers made up almost 90 per cent of all participants in the city's political disputes and 71 per cent in economic ones. The politically aware and proletarianised skilled metalworkers, therefore, remained committed to revolution.

The authorities and the employers responded to the strikes with a mixture of stick and carrot. Major disputes were broken by mobilising the strikers en masse into the army, or with threats to put the plant under military discipline. Yet employers showed more readiness than before the war to make concessions or compromises in protests of an economic nature, especially as the majority concerned demands for wage rises. The forces of law and order in fact coped relatively satisfactorily with strikers and socialist agitators alike in 1915 and 1916. The rising economic and political disaffection of workers, soldiers and middle classes ran so deep in the cities by the start of 1917, however, that any sudden and severe interruption to food supplies threatened to trigger an uncontrollable explosion of mass discontent. This is what happened in Petrograd and Moscow in the last days of February 1917.

Conclusion

At one level the answer to the question posed by the quotation at the start of the pamphlet, *"is the peaceful renovation of the country possible?"* has to be emphatically negative. The February revolution of 1917 proved that a peaceful transformation of renovated Russia was impossible. The question must remain, however, a more open one, when the impact of the Great War is discounted. The seven brief years of peace which the constitutional monarchy enjoyed, though a very short time to judge its possibilities, do provide evidence of success as well as failure. After 1906, Russian polity and society were in transition. The opportunity had been created by the tsar's political concessions of 1905-6 for Russia to move forward.

In the political sphere there was evidence of progress. The constitution and parliament opened the way to peaceful political advance. Civil society was firmly in the process of formation, as exemplified in the development of a relatively free press, public opinion, political pluralism and public congresses. Yet the political and institutional underpinnings of the constitutional monarchy were weak and there was no guarantee of legal rights. The progress of civil society was less secure in provincial centres than in the capitals. Stolypin's gamble on the moderate conservatism of the provincial landed nobility proved a grave miscalculation, a major factor behind the failure of his political reforms and his political alliance with the Octobrists. The fragmentation of Duma politics and of society at large meant that the new state structure was inherently unstable. The growing political deadlock between 1912 and 1914, for which Nicholas II must bear a share of the blame, attested to the reopening of the gulf between state and society.

The ultimate threat to political stabilisation lay in the countryside. In this area, on the eve of the Great War, the economic balance at least was more favourable. The Stolypin reforms were beginning to win over peasants to land reorganisation in their revised format of partial or complete consolidation of strips by groups of individuals or whole villages. The rural economy enjoyed an unprecedented boom, whilst peasant living standards rose, but the success concealed both economic and political flaws. The agrarian reforms signally failed to make an impact on the endemic problems of the Central Black Earth and Volga provinces. The original political goals of satisfying peasant land hunger and recovering peasant loyalty to the monarchy were not achieved, as the 1917 peasant movement would show.

If the countryside remained peaceful in 1914, the prospect for urban social stability was less promising. As the strike waves of 1912 - 14 and the apparent revival of Bolshevik fortunes would sug-

Opekushin's colossal bronze statue of Tsar Alexander III near the Church of the Redeemer
Popperfoto

gest, the working class had not been pacified. The employers and the political authorities both failed to create a new system of industrial relations, thus maintaining the exclusion of workers from civil society. There existed a core of labour and revolutionary activists, urbanised skilled male workers and worker intellectuals, who were irreconcilable to the regime.

Nonetheless, it would be incorrect to deduce from the political crisis and the labour disputes of the immediate pre-war years that the monarchy would face a new revolution like that of February 1917, let alone October 1917. Its heterogeneous opponents were unable to unite for a new assault, as they had done briefly in October 1905. The liberals were politically fragmented, divorced from workers and peasants, and organisationally and financially bankrupt. They were unable to fashion an effective response to mounting reaction. There existed no single, strong opposition among the nationalities: with the exception of Poles and Finns, none of them wanted outright independence. There was no overt peasant movement. The divisions among and within the revolutionary parties, and the frailties both of legal labour institutions and the underground cells, meant that the revolutionaries were in no position to guide working-class protest into organised channels. The army remained loyal.

If the monarchy was in no immediate danger at home in the summer of 1914, the international crisis of July 1914 and its aftermath revealed only too clearly that in the last resort the survival of the regime was tied to the maintenance of peace in Europe. Unfortunately for the monarchy, Russia's involvement in Great Power politics could not be shrugged off. The war proved beyond doubt that, in the absence of lasting and acceptable solutions to the existing tensions in the political and social framework, the regime had failed to find permanent support either in the surviving estates or the emergent social classes. In these circumstances, the First World War broke the back of the constitutional monarchy.

The record of the regime in the war was better than has been generally recognised. The military shortcomings and disasters of 1915 were remedied in large part in 1916. The army's combat fitness was restored. The bureaucracy rather than voluntary organisations was relatively successful in mobilising the economy, both industrial and agrarian, for war production. Yet, these very achievements paradoxically hastened the monarchy's demise. The rapid expansion of the officer corps undermined its loyalty by changing its social composition. The training garrisons in the rear created highly dangerous bastions of resentment. The contraction of the civilian economy, the expansion of the cities and the labour force, the methods of war finance and the unbearable strain placed upon the transport system, all exacerbated pre-existent political and social tensions among every social class. Nicholas II's outwitting of the Progressive Bloc in 1915 brought him short-term political benefits, but in the longer term only focused elite discontent directly upon the dynasty. The result was that in the last week of February 1917, as in the middle of October 1905, all social and political groups, despite their mutually incompatible objectives, could unite in a temporary coalition to overthrow tsardom.

Notes

[1] *Fraktsiia Progressistov v IVoi Gos.Dume. Sessiia 1. 1912-13gg.* (St Petersburg, 1914) I. f. 14.

[2] A fine guide to the late imperial bureaucracy is provided by **D. Lieven, *Russia's Rulers under the Old Regime*** (New Haven, CT, 1989).

[3] Two excellent guides to the army down to 1917 are **J. Bushnell, *Mutiny amid Repression: Russian Soldiers in the Revolution of 1905-6*** (Bloomington, IN, 1985) and **W. F. Fuller, Jr., *Civil-Military Conflict in Imperial Russia, 1881-1917*** (Princeton, NJ, 1985).

[4] The older interpretation of the fate of the nobility after 1861 may be found in **G. T. Robinson, *Rural Russia under the Old Regime*** (New York, 1932). A classic modern refutation of Robinson is **S. Becker, *Nobility and Privilege in Late Imperial Russia*** (De Kalb, IL, 1985).

[5] The two best introductions to the Russian Orthodox Church are: **S. M. Dixon, *Church, State and Society in Late Imperial Russia. The Diocese of St Petersburg, 1880-1914*** (London, Ph.D., 1993) and **G. L. Freeze, *The Parish Clergy in Nineteenth Century Russia. Crisis, Reform, Counter-Reform*** (Princeton, NJ, 1983).

[6] The best introduction to the comparatively neglected topic of the Russian middle class is **E. Clowes, S. D. Kassow and J. L. West (eds.), *Between Tsar and People. Educated Society and the Quest for Public Identity in Late Imperial Russia*** (Princeton, NJ, 1991).

[7] The former standard interpretation of the agrarian crisis is provided by **A. Gerschenkron, 'Agrarian Politics and Industrialisation in Russia, 1861-1917', *Cambridge Economic History*,** Volume 6, Part II, chapter eight (Cambridge 1965). The challenge to Gerschenkron comes from **P. R. Gregory, *Russian National Income, 1885-1914*** (Cambridge, 1982).

[8] The major work on the making of the constitutional monarchy is an unpublished doctoral dissertation: **G. S. Doctorow, *The Introduction of Parliamentary Institutions in Russia during the Revolution of 1905-7*** (Columbia, NY, Ph.D., 1975).

[9] The complications of the electoral law of 3 June 1907 are clearly explained in **A. Levin, *The Third Duma. Election and Profile*** (Hamden, CT, 1973).

[10] **F. W. Wcislo, *Reforming Rural Russia. State, Local Society and National Politics, 1855-1914*** (Princeton, NJ, 1990), p.232.

[11] The best studies of Stolypin's local government reforms are: Wcislo, *Reforming Rural Russia* and N. B. Weissman, *Reform in Tsarist Russia: The State Bureaucracy and Local Government, 1900-14* (New Brunswick, NJ, 1981).

[12] B. C. Pinchuk, *The Octobrists in the Third State Duma* (Seattle, OR, 1974).

[13] R. Edelman, *Gentry Politics on the Eve of the Russian Revolution: The Nationalist Party, 1907-17* (New Brunswick, NJ, 1980).

[14] A more extended version of the sections on social fragmentation and civil society may be found in R. B. McKean, 'Constitutional Russia', *Revolutionary Russia*, vol. 9 (June 1996), pp.33-42.

[15] A. J. Rieber, *Merchants and Entrepreneurs in Imperial Russia* (Chapel Hill, NC, 1982).

[16] A good review of the regime's nationality policies between 1907 and 1914 is provided by H-D. Lowe, 'Russian Nationalism and Tsarist Nationalities Policies in Semi-Constitutional Russia, 1905-14' in *New Perspectives in Russian History*, ed. R. B. McKean (London, 1992).

[17] H-D. Lowe, *The Tsars and the Jews: Reform, Reaction and Anti-Semitism in Imperial Russia, 1771-1917* (Chur, Switz., 1993) and P. R. Waldron, 'Stolypin and Finland', *Slavonic and East European Review*, 63, (1, 1985), pp.41-55.

[18] Significant recent studies of Stolypin's agrarian reforms include: D. Atkinson, *The End of the Russian Land Commune, 1905-30* (Stanford, CA, 1983): D. A. J. Macey, *Government and Peasant in Russia, 1861-1906. The Pre-History of the Stolypin Reforms* (De Kalb, IL, 1987) and G. L. Yaney, *The Urge to Mobilise. Agrarian Reform in Russia, 1861-1930* (Urbana, IL, 1982).

[19] Contrasting interpretations of the relationship between workers and revolutionaries in the years 1907 to 1914 are provided by: V. E. Bonnell, *Roots of Rebellion: Workers' Politics and Organisations in St Petersburg and Moscow, 1900-14* (Berkeley, CA, 1983); R. B. McKean, *St Petersburg between the Revolutions: Workers and Revolutionaries, June 1907 - February 1917* (New Haven, CT, 1990); and G. R. Swain, *Russian Social Democracy and the Legal Labour Movement, 1906-14* (London, 1983).

[20] In addition to Fuller, *Civil-Military Conflict*, P. Gatrell, *Government, Industry and Rearmament in Russia, 1900-1914* (Cambridge, 1994) is very useful.

[21] On Russian foreign policy between 1907 and 1914, see the specialist monographs by: W. C. Fuller, *Strategy and Power in Russia, 1600-1914* (New York, 1992); and D. M. McDonald, *United Government and Foreign Policy in Russia, 1900-1914* (Cambridge, MA, 1992).

[22] Classic statements of the older interpretation are: M. T. Florinsky, *The End of the Russian Empire* (New York, 1961

edition [first published 1931]) and **N. N. Golovine,** *The Russian Army in the World War,* (New Haven, CT, 1931).

[23] The best modern reappraisal of the army's performance in the Great War is: **D. R. Jones,** 'Imperial Russia's Forces at War', in *Military Effectiveness. Volume 1: The First World War,* ed. **A. R. Millet and W. Murray** (Boston, MA, 1988).

[24] **D. R. Jones,** 'Nicholas II and the Supreme Command: An Investigation of Motives', *Sbornik,* 11 (1985), pp. 47-83.

Further Reading

Any guide to further reading must begin with the splendid bibliographical aid to works in English covering the period provided by **Murray Frame (ed.)**, *The Russian Revolution, 1905-1921. A Bibliographic Guide to Works in English* (Westport, CT, 1995). Students will also find invaluable and informative the collection of documents edited by **George Vernadsky**, *A Source Book for Russian History from Early Times to 1917. Volume 3. Alexander II to the February Revolution* (New Haven, CT, 1972).

Three recently published general studies will serve as introductions to the late tsarist period. These are: **O. Figes**, *A People's Tragedy. The Russian Revolution, 1891-1924* (London, 1996); **W. E. Mosse**, *Perestroika Under the Tsars* (London, 1992); **R. Pipes**, *The Russian Revolution, 1899-1919* (London, 1990).

The modern debate on the fate of 'Renovated Russia' after 1905 was launched by **L. H. Haimson's** celebrated article 'The Problem of Social Stability in Urban Russia, 1905-1917 (Part One), *Slavic Review*, 23 (4, 1964), pp.61-42, and 'The Problem of Social Stability in Urban Russia, 1905-1917 (Part Two)', *Slavic Review*, 24 (1, 1965), pp. 1-22, as well as the replies to Haimson in *Slavic Review* by **Th. Von Laue, A. Levin, A. P. Mendel,** and **G. L. Yaney**. It was then taken up by **T. G. Stavrou and G. Katkov (ed.)**, *Russia Under the Last Tsar* (Minneapolis, 1969) and by **G. Katkov**, *Russia Enters the Twentieth Century* (London, 1971). The present author's earlier Historical Association pamphlet, *The Russian Constitutional Monarchy, 1907-17,* (1977) provides a guide to the outlines of the debate as it had evolved between 1964 and 1976. Readers of the present work will be able to note the significant changes in interpretation in the light of research since the late 1970s. Four stimulating collections of essays which summarise much research on late imperial society and politics after 1905 are: **E. Clowes, S. D. Kassow, J. L. West (eds.)**, *Between Tsar and People. Educated Society and the Quest for Public Identity in Late Imperial Russia* (Princeton, NJ, 1991); **O. Crisp and L. Edmondson (eds.)**, *Civil Rights in Imperial Russia* (Oxford, 1989); **R. B. McKean**, *New Perspectives in Russian History* (London, 1992); and **T. Taranovski (ed.)**, *Reform in Modern Russian History. Progress or Cycle?* (Cambridge 1995).

The social history of the late tsarist Russia has received much scholarly attention in the last two decades. On the nobility, two works are of particular value: **R. T. Manning**, *The Crisis of the Old Order in Russia. Gentry and Gov-*

ernment (Princeton, NJ, 1982) and D. Lieven, *The Aristocracy in Europe, 1815-1914* (London, 1992). As to the peasantry, three collections of essays by the foremost authorities in the field stand out: R. Bartlett (ed.), *Land Commune and Peasant Community in Russia. Communal Forms in Imperial and Early Soviet History* (London, 1990); B. Eklof and S. P. Frank (eds.), *The World of the Russian Peasant. Post-Emancipation Culture and Society* (London 1990); and E. Kingston-Mann and T. Mixter (eds.), *Peasant Economy, Culture and Politics of European Russia, 1800-1921* (Princeton, NJ, 1991). Concerning the attitudes of Russia's elites to the emergent working class, T. McDaniel, *Autocracy, Capitalism and Revolution in Russia* (Berkeley, CA, 1988) is indispensible.

The revolution of 1905 receives thorough treatment in two volumes of A. Ascher, *The Revolution of 1905. Russia in Disarray* (Stanford, CA, 1988) and *The Revolution of 1905. Authority Restored* (Stanford, CA, 1992). A most helpful translation of and commentary upon the revised Fundamental State Laws of 1906 comes from M. Szeftel, *The Russian Constitution of 23 April 1906. Political Institutions of the Duma Monarchy* (Brussels, 1976).

No evaluation of the reign of the last tsar can ignore Nicholas II's personality and role in high politics. Two contrasting interpretations are provided by D. Lieven, *Nicholas II: Emperor of All the Russias* (London, 1993) and by A. M. Verner, *The Crisis of Autocracy. Nicholas II and the 1905 Revolution* (Princeton, NJ, 1990).

The best general surveys of Stolypin's term of office are provided by: M. S.

Conroy, *Petr Arkad'evich Stolypin. Practical Politics in Late Tsarist Russia* (Boulder, CO, 1976); G. Hosking, *The Russian Constitutional Experiment: Government and Duma, 1907-14* (Cambridge, 1973); and P. R. Waldron, *Between the Revolutions. Stolypin and the Politics of Renewal in Russia* (1988). The debate on the pre-conditions for civil society can be followed in E. Clowes, S. D. Kassow, J. L. West (eds.), *Between Tsar and People. Educated Society and the Quest for Public Identity in Late Imperial Russia* (Princeton, NJ, 1991).

Three essential surveys of the conomy, both rural and urban, on the eve of the First World War are: R. W. Davies (ed.), *From Tsarism to the New Economic Policy. Continuity or Change in the Economy of the USSR* (London, 1990); and P. Gatrell, *The Tsarist Economy, 1850-1917* (London, 1986); P. R. Gregory, *Russian National Income, 1885-1913* (Cambridge, 1982). On Russian foreign policy before and after 1907, consult D. Geyer, *Russian Imperialism. The Interaction of Domestic and Foreign Policy, 1860-1914* (Leamington Spa, 1987) and D. Lieven, *Russia and the Origins of the First World War* (London, 1983).

The impact of the First World War upon the Russian army is traced by N. Stone, *The Eastern Front* (London, 1975). Reinterpretations of the war economy may be found in: P. Gatrell, 'The First World War and War Communism' in *The Economic Transformation of the Soviet Union, 1913-45*, edited by R. W. Davies, M. Harrison, S. G. Wheatcroft (Cambridge, 1994); and P. Gatrell and M.

46

Harrison, 'The Russian and Soviet Economies in Two World Wars: a Comparative View', *Economic History Review*, 46 (3,1993). On political developments, the classic, if outdated, account is: **B. Pares,** *The Fall of the Russian Monarchy* (London, 1939). A more reliable study is: **R.** Pearson, *The Russian Moderates and the Crisis of Tsarism,* *1914-1917* (London, 1977). On the labour and revolutionary movements in the war, see: **R. B.** McKean, *St Petersburg between the Revolutions. Workers and Revolutionaries, June 1907 - February 1917* (New Haven, Conn., 1990) and **M.** Melancon, *The Socialist Revolutionaries and the Russian Anti-War Movement,* *1914-17* (Columbus, OH, 1990).

About the Author

Dr McKean is Reader in History at the University of Stirling. He was educated at the universities of Glasgow, East Anglia and Leningrad. He is the author of *St Petersburg between the Revolutions. Workers and Revolutionaries, June 1907 - February 1917* (1990) and editor of *New Perspectives in Russian History* (1992).

Cover

Nicholas II's Coronation procession enters the city through the Triumphal Gate and down the Tverskaya running two miles south to the Red Square.
© *Bildarchiv Preussischer Kulturbesitz, 1896.*

H.I.M. Nicholas II, Emperor of Russia, by Bogdanow-Bielsky.
Royal Collection Enterprises.